"There Goes My Baby!"

Other For Better or For Worse® Books

For Better or For Worse: The 10th Anniversary Collection
Things Are Looking Up . . .
What, Me Pregnant?
If This Is a Lecture, How Long Will It Be?
Pushing 40
It's All Downhill From Here
Keep the Home Fries Burning
The Last Straw
Just One More Hug
It Must Be Nice to Be Little
Is This "One of Those Days," Daddy?
I've Got the One-More-Washload Blues

A *For Better or For Worse*® Collection

"There Goes My Baby!"

by Lynn Johnston

Andrews and McMeel
A Universal Press Syndicate Company
Kansas City

OH, WOW! DRIVING WITH MICHAEL IS GONNA BE **AWESOME!**

I HOPE SOMEBODY I KNOW GOES BY - I WANT PEOPLE TO SEE ME!!

LOOK! IT'S ME! ELIZABETH!! - I'M WITH MY BROTHER WHO'S 16 AND HAS AN ACTUAL DRIVER'S LICENSE!

HEY, COULD YOU DUCK DOWN A BIT, LIZ?... I DON'T WANT GUYS TO THINK I'M OUT WITH MY SISTER.

ONE ROCKY ROAD, ONE...

LOOK, MIKE - THERE'S MARTHA!

HAH! BET SHE'S SORRY SHE DUMPED YOU.. BUT WHO NEEDS HER, RIGHT? - AN WHO CARES! BESIDES... YOU'VE STILL GOT **ME!!**

HEY, LIZ... I'VE BEEN PRETTY NICE TO YOU - SO HOW ABOUT DOING ME A HUGE FAVOR!

OK.

GET LOST!!

MALL EXIT

OH, SURE! MY BROTHER DRIVES ME TO THE MALL FOR AN ICE CREAM CONE, THEN DUMPS ME WHEN HIS EX-GIRLFRIEND SHOWS UP!!

IF YOU DON'T WANNA BE WITH ME, THEN WHY DID YOU BRING ME DOWN HERE?

COME ON, LIZ... TRY AN' BE UNDER-STANDING!!!

I NEED TO, YOU KNOW - TALK TO HER. ALONE. I'LL PICK YOU UP AT THE DRUGSTORE IN AN HOUR. OK? HERE - TAKE THIS.

YOU WANT ME TO BE UNDERSTANDING FOR A BUCK?!!

HI, MARTHA! — I DIDN'T KNOW YOU WERE HERE!!

SO..HOW'S IT GOING? I HAVEN'T SEEN YOU 'ROUND!

I GUESS I'VE BEEN BUSY.

WELL, GOTTA GO.

SEE YOU.

WHY DID I DO THAT? WHY DID I CHASE HER HALFWAY 'ROUND THE MALL JUST TO SAY "HELLO"? — MAYBE I LIKE BEING DEPRESSED!

...HOW CAN I FIGURE HER OUT, WHEN I DON'T EVEN UNDERSTAND ME?!!!

AH GOT A STABBIN' IN MAH GUT! (UGH!) AN' I DUNNO WHUT (UGH!) AHMA GONNA DO, BECUZ MAH BABY GONE AN' SHUT ME OUTTTTTT

SHE SEZ SHE'S GONNA TRY (UGH!) WITH ANOTHER GUY (UGH!) I NEVAH THOUGHT SHE'D DUMP ME AN' AH DUNNO WHAT IT'S ALL ABOUTTTT

THUMPA BZANGSS BOOM

BOOM THUD

...AH GOTTA SHOUTTT KEAGHHH

{SNIFF} ...THESE SENTIMENTAL SONGS ALWAYS GET TO ME.

BOOM THUD BOOM THUD BOOM THUD BOOM THUD BOOM THUD...

I THINK WE STRUCK OUT, GORDO. THIS IS THE 3RD PLACE WE'VE BEEN, AN' ZIP IS HAPPENING!

SKRAKK

DON'T SAY THAT, MIKE! I'VE BEEN CHECKIN' OUT THE BABE BEHIND THE COUNTER... AN' SHE'S BEEN LOOKIN' AT US KINDA INTERESTED, LIKE!!

SPPTT

LOOK!! SHE'S COMIN' OVER, MAN! WHAT DID I TELL YOU! AN'... SHE'S GOT THAT "LOOK".—THE ONE THAT SAYS.....

SPTTT

I FORGOT TO GIVE YOU A NEW KETCHUP SQUEEZER... SOME KID WAS SUCKIN' ON THIS ONE.

IT'S AFTER 10!... I WONDER WHERE MICHAEL IS.

PROBABLY CRUISIN'.

WHAT?!!

CRUISIN! —THAT'S WHAT WE USED TO DO. WE'D PILE GUYS INTO DAD'S OLD CHEVY, AND DRIVE AROUND TOWN LOOKING FOR GIRLS!

WE'D HANG OUT THE WINDOWS, AND YELL "HEY, BABY, WANNA RIDE?" AND STUFF LIKE THAT.

WELL, HOPEFULLY, IN THIS DAY AND AGE, THE BOYS HAVE A LITTLE MORE CLASS!

OOGA OOGA OOGH!

WELL, WE HIT A NEGATIVE ON BABES, MAN.

BUT IT WAS A GREAT NIGHT, GORD.

CLICK!

KNOW WHAT?—THERE'S NOTHING LIKE BEIN' OUT WITH THE GUYS! GUYS ARE SOLID. NO HASSLES, NO GAMES—YOU CAN BURRP.... BE COMPLETELY YOURSELF!

BUT BABES? THEY CAN EITHER BE GREAT, OR THEY CAN MAKE YOU CRAZY. THEY CAN CHEW YOU UP AN' SPIT YOU OUT. THEY CAN MASH YOU INTO THE DIRT LIKE ROADKILL!

.... I WAS WILLING TO TAKE THE RISK.

OH..... I THOUGHT YOU SAID WE WERE HAVING STEAK WITH FRIES!!

LOOK, LIZ... I'VE GOT A MOSQUITO ON MY ARM!

SMACK IT!!

IT'S A FEMALE.. ONLY FEMALES NEED BLOOD! SEE? SHE'S PUTTING HER NEEDLE IN.

SMACK IT SMACK IT!

WATCH HER ABDOMEN AS SHE...

AACH!

SMAK!

ONCE AGAIN... THERE'S NO SUCH THING AS A FREE LUNCH.

DO THESE STEAKS LOOK READY?

I THINK SO.

CHECK OUT THE INSIDE – ARE THEY JUST RIGHT?

THEY'RE READY, DAD.

ARE YOU SURE THEY'RE READY?

ALL READY!

DON'T COOK THE STEAKS YET... DINNER'S NOT READY!!

IS IT THAT TIME ALREADY? UH-HUH... GRAM AND GRAMP'S NEW CONDOMINIUM IS ALL READY FOR THEM.

UNCLE PHIL IS GOING TO PICK ME UP SOON. WE SHOULD BE IN VANCOUVER BY 3 O'CLOCK.

I WISH I COULD COME.

YOU WOULDN'T HAVE ANY FUN, LIZ. MOVING IS HARD WORK, AND WE'LL BE SORTING THROUGH 40 YEARS OF STUFF!

JUST MOVING MOM'S CANNING JARS ALONE COULD TAKE A WEEK!!

I TALKED TO DAD LAST NIGHT, EL. THEIR NEW PLACE SOUNDS PRETTY SMALL; THEY WON'T BE ABLE TO TAKE MUCH WITH THEM.

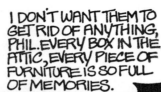

I DON'T WANT THEM TO GET RID OF ANYTHING, PHIL. EVERY BOX IN THE ATTIC, EVERY PIECE OF FURNITURE IS SO FULL OF MEMORIES.

YEAH. IT WOULD BE LIKE SAYING GOODBYE TO OUR CHILDHOOD. I WONDER HOW THE FOLKS FEEL ABOUT IT.

WELL, HON? WHAT WILL WE DO WITH ALL THIS JUNK?!

WE'LL HAVE TO GET SPACE IN A MOVING VAN IF WE WANT TO BRING THE BIG THINGS HOME, EL.

RIGHT.

SO, IS THERE ANYTHING YOU REALLY WANT? I MEAN, WE'RE DIVIDING UP HEIRLOOMS HERE. PERHAPS WE SHOULD DISCUSS IT NOW.

I WANT THE PUMP ORGAN.

THE PUMP ORGAN? BUT WE SETTLED THAT!! I'VE ALWAYS THOUGHT I'D GET THE PUMP ORGAN!

WHY?

...IT JUST WENT WITHOUT SAYING!

SOMETIMES, THINGS THAT "GO WITHOUT SAYING" OUGHT TO BE SAID!!!

WE'RE ON OUR WAY TO HELP OUR PARENTS MOVE OUT OF THE HOUSE THEY'VE LIVED IN FOR 40 YEARS, AND WE ARE ARGUING!!

WE ARE NOT ARGUING.

WE ARE TALKING ABOUT THE FACT THAT YOU'VE PUT DIBS ON SOMETHING THAT BELONGS TO ME.

THE PUMP ORGAN DOES NOT BELONG TO YOU, EL.

EVER SINCE WE WERE KIDS, PHIL, YOU'VE HAD YOUR OWN WAY!

RIGHT! HERE WE GO AGAIN! LOOK, EL—IT'S ABOUT TIME YOU...

COFFEE? TEA? ...IMPARTIAL ARBITRATION?

GRUMBLE, SNARL...

CAROUSEL 3

GRUMBLE, SNARL, GNASH, FUME, SNORT.

ELLY! PHIL! YOU'RE HERE!!

THE FAMILY'S TOGETHER AGAIN!!

AND ISN'T IT NICE FOR YOU TO BE LIKE "BROTHER AND SISTER" AGAIN!

WELL, MOTHER AND I HAVE STARTED TO PACK... WHAT WE DON'T TAKE TO THE NEW HOUSE CAN BE DIVIDED BETWEEN YOU.

THE PUMP ORGAN IS MINE!!

IF PHIL GETS THE PUMP ORGAN, THERE'LL BE FIREWORKS!

...I'M SURE YOU'VE BOTH DECIDED WHAT YOU WANT.

ONE THING YOU'LL BE PLEASED ABOUT—WE WON'T HAVE TO WRESTLE WITH THAT OLD PUMP ORGAN!

.....I GAVE IT TO THE CHURCH LAST WEEK!!!

I GUESS WE'RE ALL MOVED IN!

BUT, DEAR--THERE'S STILL SO MUCH LEFT AT THE HOUSE!

PHIL AND I HAVE CALLED A MOVING VAN, MOM. WE'RE TAKING THE REST OF YOUR FURNITURE HOME WITH US.

AND WE'RE GOING TO HAVE A YARD SALE!-- REMEMBER ALL THE THINGS WE PRICED AND PUT ASIDE?!

OH. YES. I THINK SO.

YOU'RE FORGETTING THINGS, MOM!

MAYBE I JUST DON'T WANT TO REMEMBER.

OUR HOUSE IS EMPTY.

IT DOESN'T SEEM REAL, DOES IT!

I HOPE THE NEW OWNERS LOVE IT AS MUCH AS WE DID. I HOPE THEY KEEP THE GARDEN AND FEED THE BIRDS AND HAVE BREAKFAST ON THE PORCH IN THE SUMMER!

WILL OUR CONDOMINIUM EVER BE "HOME" TO YOU, DEAR?

OF COURSE IT WILL, MOM!

... BECAUSE **YOU'RE** THERE!

SEE YOU IN THE MORNING, MOM AND DAD! HAVE A GOOD NIGHT IN YOUR NEW HOME!

LOOK AT US, MARIAN. SUDDENLY WE'VE GONE FROM LIVING IN A BIG 3-BEDROOM HOUSE TO A TINY PLACE WITH JUST THE BARE ESSENTIALS!

IT'S A STRANGE FEELING, ISN'T IT.

YES....

... I FEEL LIKE A NEWLYWED AGAIN!!!

EEEEEWWWW ULGKKK Yuck!!

DAD! MICHAEL PUT KETCHUP IN HIS MOUTH AN' LET IT DRIP OUT LIKE BLOOD!!

GROSS!! EEWW! — THAT WAS TOTALLY, TOTALLY **GROSS**!!

...DO IT AGAIN!

WHEN ARE MOM AN' UNCLE PHIL COMING HOME, DAD? AS SOON AS GRANDMA AND GRANDPA ARE SETTLED INTO THEIR CONDOMINIUM.

I WISH MOM WAS HERE.

ME TOO.

THE PLACE JUST ISN'T THE SAME WITHOUT HER.

MICHAEL, GET THE LAUNDRY DONE! LIZ-FINISH THE DISHES! THIS PLACE IS A **DISASTER**! — WHAT WOULD YOUR MOTHER SAY IF SHE SAW IT LIKE THIS?!

AWW, DAD! THERE ARE THREE CAPABLE PEOPLE HERE · GIVE ME ONE GOOD REASON WHY WE SHOULDN'T CLEAN UP THIS PLACE RIGHT **NOW**!

MOM WON'T BE HOME UNTIL MONDAY!

GOOD ENOUGH.

KNOW WHAT I'D LIKE TO DO BEFORE WE LEAVE VANCOUVER, EL? SWING ON THE SUSPENSION BRIDGE, VISIT THE OLD SCHOOL, AND WATCH THE FERRY DOCK AT HORSESHOE BAY.

I WANT TO SEE SOME OLD FRIENDS, RIDE THE CHAIRLIFT, WALK AROUND STANLEY PARK... AND BUY A HOT DOG AT THE ZOO!!

WE'LL BE BACK IN A FEW HOURS, MOM. PHIL AND I WANT TO RELIVE A FEW SCENES FROM OUR CHILDHOOD!

THAT'S NICE, DEAR.

DRIVE CAREFULLY, HAVE SOMETHING GOOD FOR LUNCH, AND CALL IF YOU'LL BE HOME LATER THAN 9.

THE OLD CEDAR VUE THEATRE USED TO BE ON THAT CORNER, EL. NOW IT'S A MALL.

...AND HOW COULD THEY TEAR DOWN OUR SCHOOL?

THAT WHOLE HILLSIDE USED TO BE FOREST. NOW IT'S A HUGE HOUSING DEVELOPMENT!

EVERYTHING'S DIFFERENT.

I GUESS WHAT THEY SAY IS TRUE: "YOU CAN NEVER GO HOME AGAIN."

OH, YOU CAN GO HOME AGAIN....

...BUT IT FEELS AS THOUGH SOMEBODY'S CHANGED THE LOCKS!!

GOODBYE. THANK YOU FOR ALL YOUR HELP, DEAR.

AND DON'T YOU WORRY ABOUT US... WE'LL BE FINE!

DO YOU REALLY THINK THEY'LL BE O K, PHIL?

I HOPE SO. I'LL ASK THE COUSINS TO LOOK IN ON THEM.

STRANGE HOW THE ROLES HAVE BEEN REVERSED, ISN'T IT. WE'RE BECOMING PARENTS TO OUR PARENTS.

I KNOW.

...AND I'M NOT READY TO STOP BEING THE CHILD!!

21

24

ONE, TWO, THREE....
WHEEEEE!!

SHRIEK!

ONE, TWO, THREE...
WHEEE...

ONE, TWO, THREE..
WHEEEE!

MOM, WE WANNA GO TO THE STORE—CAN I HAVE SOME MONEY?

I GUESS SO.

WHAT DID I DO THAT FOR? ELIZABETH SHOULD HAVE EARNED THAT MONEY!! I'M NOT DOING HER A FAVOR BY GIVING IT TO HER!!

WHY DON'T I THINK FIRST? WHAT EXAMPLE AM I SETTING? WHY AM I SO INCONSISTENT? —WHAT KIND OF PARENT AM I?!!

....AMAZING HOW THE MOST DEVASTATING LECTURES ARE THE ONES YOU GIVE YOURSELF!

ELIZABETH, BEFORE YOU GO TO THE STORE, I WANT TO REMIND YOU THAT YOUR ROOM NEEDS CLEANING, AND YOU STILL HAVE TO FOLD THE LAUNDRY.

ALSO, THE DOG NEEDS BRUSHING, AND THERE'S A VOLLEYBALL NET IN THE BASEMENT THAT HAS TO GO BACK TO ANNE'S.

OH, AND WHILE I THINK OF IT, YOUR BICYCLE WASN'T PUT AWAY LAST NIGHT, YOU FORGOT TO TURN THE TV OFF, AND YOUR SOCKS ARE STILL IN THE STAIRWELL...

EVERY TIME MOM GOES AWAY FOR A WHILE...SHE HAS TO CATCH UP ON HER NAGGING!

OOH-OW-OOOCH-OUCH!! WALK SLOWER, DAWN! THERE'S STONES ON THE SIDEWALK!

HOW COME YOU'RE NOT WEARING SHOES?

I FORGOT.

THEN, I GUESS THERE'S ONLY ONE THING WE CAN DO...

OOH OW! OOH

OOH OUCH! OW!

KNOW WHAT, LIZ? SOMEWHERE, RIGHT NOW, ON THIS EARTH ARE THE TWO GUYS WE'RE GONNA MARRY!

THEY DON'T KNOW WHO WE ARE... AN' WE DON'T KNOW THEM, BUT SOMEDAY DESTINY WILL BRING US TOGETHER AN' WE'LL FALL IN LOVE!

WHO KNOWS WHAT THEY LOOK LIKE, WHO KNOWS WHAT THEY'LL BE!—AN' THE AMAZING THING IS—WE MIGHT EVEN HAVE MET THEM ALREADY!!!

..... I DON'T LIKE TO THINK ABOUT IT.

DESTINY IS COOL, DAWN. IF YOU HADN'T MOVED ACROSS THE STREET, WE MIGHT NEVER HAVE MET!

YEAH!—AN' IF OUR PARENTS NEVER MET, WE'D NEVER HAVE BEEN BORN—SO, WE WERE **MEANT** TO BE, ELIZABETH. WE WERE SUPPOSED TO MEET!!

THERE'S A REASON STUFF HAPPENS!—AN' YOU AN' I, IN THIS PLACE, AT THIS TIME IN OUR LIVES, WERE DESTINED TO COME TOGETHER!!

AWE-SOME!

I GUESS IT'S A GOOD THING WE **LIKE** EACH OTHER!

YEAH! A GOOD THING!

For Better or For Worse

By Lynn Johnston

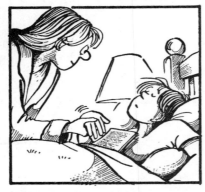

HEY, DAWN! CANDACE! CHECK OUT THESE GREAT FELT PENS.—I'M GONNA GET SOME FOR SCHOOL.

YAH!

I WONDER HOW THEY WRITE....THERE ISN'T ANY PAPER.

BACK TO SCHOOL

WE HAD TO TRY THEM OUT ON SOMETHING!!

GRAWKKKKKK

GRAWWKKKKKK

SLRK SLRK SLURKK SWUURRRKKK

SLRK SLRK, SWRK SLUURRRKKKK

SLOOO OOOOOO OOOOOO OOOO RPPPP

SLOOOO OOOOOO OOOORP

I ALWAYS WONDERED WHY KIDS DID THAT.... —IT'S A MATING CALL.

I DID ALL MY SCHOOL SHOPPING, MOM...AN' I GOT EVERYTHING ON THE LIST!

SEE? I KNOW HOW TO BUY MY OWN CLOTHES. I KNOW WHAT'S SENSIBLE AND WHAT ISN'T..AND I CAN KEEP TRACK OF ALL THE MONEY I SPEND!

SHOES

YOU WERE RIGHT, LIZ. YOU DON'T NEED ME WITH YOU ANY MORE. YOU DID A VERY GOOD JOB.

I KNOW.

—I HAD A VERY GOOD TEACHER.

For Better or For Worse
By Lynn Johnston

HI, NANDINI? IT'S ALL SETTLED! DAWN, AN' IRIS AN' CANDACE AN' MEG ALL WANNA WEAR THE SAME THING!

I DUNNO. THEY SAID THEY'D WEAR WHATEVER I WANNA WEAR! ...... SO, WHAT DO YOU WANNA WEAR?

YEAH! WE SIT TOGETHER IN ENGLISH AN' FRENCH, SO WHY DON'T WE ALL WEAR CUT-OFFS AN' RED T'S! - THAT WOULD BE TOTALLY COOL!

DID YOU KNOW THAT KYLE MCNAIR'S LOCKER IS NEXT TO MINE? - HOOOO WHAT A BABE!!

YOU GONNA DO YOUR NAILS? WHAT COLOR? - IF YOU PUT ON TOO MANY LAYERS, IT'LL CHIP WHEN YOU TAKE GYM.

I PUT ON EYESHADOW THE OTHER DAY, AN' YOU KNOW HOW MR. LUCAS TOTALLY HATES MAKE UP? WELL, I WENT INTO MATH CLASS AN' HE GOES...

ELIZABETH!

YOU HAVE ALL KINDS OF WORK TO DO - AND HERE YOU ARE - TALKING ON THE PHONE FOR HALF THE EVENING!!!

BUT, MOM... IT'S ABOUT **SCHOOL**!!

DON'T WORRY ABOUT MY LUNCH, MOM - I MADE IT!

I'M CATCHING THE EARLY BUS! - 'BYE!

ISN'T IT NICE TO SEE THE KIDS BACK IN SCHOOL, ANNE?... NEW FRIENDS, NEW PLANS - IT'S A WHOLE NEW BEGINNING!

NOW I CAN GET MY HOUSE IN ORDER!

NOW I CAN WORK ON A REGULAR SCHEDULE. THIS IS WHEN EVERYTHING RETURNS TO NORMAL.

- WHO SAYS THE "NEW YEAR" BEGINS IN JANUARY!!

THIS IS WICKED! WE ARE IN A TOTALLY NEW SCHOOL THIS YEAR!!

DID YOU FIND YOUR LOCKER?

YEAH. IT'S NEXT TO THE GYM.

DID YOU SEE THE GYM?

IT'S HUGE! - AN' CHECK THE EQUIPMENT!!

THE CAFETERIA IS AMAZING!

SO IS THE SCIENCE LAB!

EVERYTHING LOOKS FANTASTIC!

AND, JUST THINK, GUYS... IN A FEW MONTHS, WE'LL HATE THIS PLACE!!

WHO DO YOU HAVE FOR ENGLISH?

MR. ALLEN.

ME TOO. I WONDER WHAT HE'S LIKE.

THE BEST THING ABOUT BEING IN A NEW SCHOOL WITH NEW TEACHERS IS... NOBODY KNOWS WHAT YOU'RE LIKE!

YEAH! THE SLATE'S CLEAN! WHATEVER WE DID LAST YEAR IS HISTORY!

ACTUALLY, I THINK I GET YOU FOR MATH!

MISS EDWARDS!!

TO MY BRIDE OF 43 YEARS: I TOAST THEE, FAIR LADY... AND, PRAY THAT WE HAVE MANY MORE HAPPY YEARS TOGETHER!

IT'S BEEN A GOOD LIFE, JIM.

IT'S STILL A GOOD LIFE! LOOK AT US! WE'RE AS YOUNG AT HEART AS WE'VE EVER BEEN!!

WE'RE YOUNG AND IN LOVE AND WE CAN STILL BOOGIE WITH THE BEST!!

WHAT ARE YOU DRINKING?

....METAMUCIL, STRAIGHT UP.

IS IT GRANDMA AN' GRANDPA'S ANNIVERSARY TODAY?

UH HUH. THEY'VE BEEN MARRIED FOR 43 YEARS.

43 YEARS - TO THE SAME PERSON. THAT'S AWESOME!

YES IT IS, IN TODAY'S SOCIETY.

TODAY, PEOPLE DON'T PUT UP WITH THINGS THE WAY THEY USED TO. DIVORCE HAS BECOME COMMONPLACE. -THAT'S JUST THE WAY IT IS.

HANG IN THERE!!

YOU EVER GONNA GET MARRIED, DAWN?

MAYBE.

BUT IT WON'T BE FOR A LONG, LONG TIME. FIRST I'M GOING TO DO EVERYTHING IN MY WHOLE LIFE THAT I EVER WANTED TO DO.

LIKE WHAT?

I DON'T KNOW.

....THAT'S WHY I'M NOT GONNA GET MARRIED FOR A LONG, LONG TIME.

For Better or For Worse

By Lynn Johnston

"I'D SAY YOU'RE DOING PRETTY WELL WITH YOUR DRIVING, MIKE!"

"THANKS!"

"... MIND IF I BORROW YOUR CAR?"

"OH, WOW!! - THANKS, DAD!"

"WHAT'S GOING ON?"

"- I'M LETTING MIKE DRIVE MY CAR."

"I CAN'T BELIEVE MY SON HAS HIS LICENCE ALREADY."

"WHAT AM I DOING?... NOBODY DRIVES THAT CAR BUT ME!"

"IT SEEMS LIKE YESTERDAY... HE WAS SO LITTLE... RIDING HIS TRICYCLE!"

"WATCH THE GEARS!! PLEASE!..."

"WATCH THE GEARS!!"

VROOMMM

"... THERE GOES MY BABY!!!"

For Better or For Worse By Lynn Johnston

MOM? CAN I SIGN UP FOR THE DRAMA CLUB? THEY MEET EVERY WEDNESDAY.

OH, AN' MIKE SAYS HE WANTS TO START BOWLING!

NOW... LET ME GET THIS STRAIGHT: MONDAY, YOU HAVE VOLLEYBALL PRACTICE, AND MIKE GOES TO HOCKEY. TUESDAY YOU HAVE CHOIR AND MIKE HAS COMPUTER CLUB....

WEDNESDAY, HE SIGNED UP FOR C.P.R. AND HAS TO BE DRIVEN TO THE COLLEGE CAMPUS....

THURSDAYS YOU SKATE; ON FRIDAY, YOU BOTH GO TO THE Y....

WEEKENDS ARE CRAZY— AND NOW YOU'RE TALKING ABOUT DRAMA CLUB AND BOWLING?!!!

ELIZABETH, EVER SINCE SCHOOL STARTED, THERE'S BEEN SOMETHING GOING ON EVERY SINGLE MINUTE!

I KNOW....

—ISN'T IT NICE TO GET BACK INTO A ROUTINE?!!

47

OH, WOW. I CAN'T BELIEVE I'M STAYING HOME TONIGHT BECAUSE OF A LOUSY **ZIT**!!!

I MUST BE THE MOST CONCEITED, SELF-CENTERED.....

WHACK!

HI, MIKE. HOW COME YOU'RE NOT GOING TO THE DANCE?

...I HURT MY FOOT.

I HOPE YOU'RE NOT TOO DISAPPOINTED THAT MIKE COULDN'T TAKE YOU TO THE DANCE TONIGHT, TRACE.

IT'S OK.

ONCE WE GET THERE, YOU DON'T HAFTA STAY WITH ME. I KNOW YOU LIKE MARTIN BEAN, SO YOU DON'T EVEN HAFTA DRIVE HOME WITH ME IF YOU GET A BETTER OFFER.

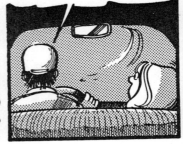

AN' IF ALLYSON'S THERE, I MIGHT GET TO SEE HER. SHE WON'T TALK TO ME, AN' SHE DEFINITELY WON'T DANCE WITH ME, BUT SHE STILL MIGHT BE THERE!!

YOU'RE INCREDIBLE, GORDON.

I LIKE TO THINK POSITIVE.

HERE I AM, ALONE IN MY ROOM WHEN I COULD HAVE BEEN AT THE DANCE. GORD AN' TRACEY ARE PROB'LY HAVING A GREAT TIME.

IT'S NO FAIR! I AM MISSING THE SOCIAL EVENT OF THE SEASON!!

BOOM THUD BOOM THUD
HI WHAT? WHO? HUH? HELLO! I CAN'T HEAR YOU! HI HUH? SAY AGAIN? WHA? HUH?
BOOM THUD BOOM THUD

HONEY, WOULD YOU GET THE PHONE?... MY HANDS ARE COVERED WITH COOKIE DOUGH!

RINGG RINGG

HELLO? NO, MIKE'S NOT HERE. HE SHOULD HAVE BEEN HERE AN HOUR AGO.

NO, I DON'T KNOW WHERE HE IS-IF I DID, I'D BE TELLING HIM TO GET HIS TAIL HOME IMMEDIATELY!!!

YOU'RE RIGHT, MIKE, YER OLD MAN'S GETTIN' TICKED.

GUESS I'LL HAFTA PACK IT IN, GUYS.

SEEMS STRANGE TO BE HANGIN' AROUND WITHOUT GORDO.

REALLY WEIRD.

HE'S ACTUALLY DATING!!

WE'VE LOST A GREAT MEMBER OF THE TEAM, GUYS.

(SIGH) WE'RE SURE GONNA MISS HIM.

THERE WAS SOMETHING SPECIAL ABOUT GORDO..... SOMETHING HARD TO REPLACE.

YEAH..... HE WAS THE ONLY GUY I KNOW WHO COULD GET WHEELS EVERY SATURDAY NIGHT.

54

I LOVE THIS TIME OF YEAR. I LOVE THE RUSTLE OF DRY LEAVES AND THE CHILL IN THE AIR.

I LOVE THE TASTE OF FRESH CORN AND PUMPKIN PIE AND THE SMELL OF WOOD FIRES BURNING!

I'M GLAD WE TOOK THE TIME TONIGHT TO APPRECIATE THIS BEAUTIFUL SEASON!

SO AM I.

I'VE BEEN SO BUSY... I ALMOST MISSED IT.

LOOK AT APRIL, HONEY- ISN'T SHE ADORABLE? SHE'S ALL READY FOR HALLOWE'EN!

JUST A FEW MORE PHOTOS IN HERE, AND THEN WE CAN SHOW HER OFF!

THAT'S IT, GO UP THE STAIRS AGAIN ...SAY "TRICK OR TREAT!" SMILE AT ANNIE! THAT'S RIGHT, UP THE STAIRS!

YESTERDAY, I WAS WALKING AROUND, PLAYING WITH THE BABY, DOING NORMAL STUFF THEN... **SNAP!!**

TODAY, I'M FLAT ON MY BACK. EVERY MOVEMENT IS AGONY!

LET THIS BE A LESSON TO YOU, MIKE. NEVER TAKE GOOD HEALTH FOR GRANTED. BE GRATEFUL YOU CAN GET OUT AND DO THINGS!

I AM, DAD.

WHICH REMINDS ME... SINCE YOU'RE NOT USING IT... COULD I BORROW YOUR CAR?

I'VE BEEN LYING HERE FOR TWO WHOLE DAYS, EL.- STRANGE HOW YOU BECOME DEEPLY PHILOSOPHICAL WHEN YOU'RE INCAPACITATED.

I'VE BEEN THINKING: "WHAT IS LIFE?" "WHAT'S IT LIKE TO DIE?" "WHAT'S MAN'S ROLE IN THIS INFINITE COSMOS?" ..."WHAT'S FOR LUNCH?"

LUNCH?

...I LIKE SOME OF MY QUESTIONS TO HAVE ANSWERS.

ELLY! I HEAR THAT YOUR HUSBAND PUT HIS BACK OUT!

UH HUH.

HE'S IN BED ALL DAY WITH ICE PACKS AND HEATING PADS, BUT NOTHING SEEMS TO MAKE HIM COMFORTABLE.

HE CAN WALK A LITTLE, BUT HE CAN'T SIT DOWN. THE DOCTOR SAYS IT COULD BE DAYS BEFORE HE STARTS FEELING BETTER.

TSK!.... YOU POOR THING.

60

I GOT UP FOR AWHILE. I WATCHED SOME TV. I ATE A BOWL OF SOUP. I WENT TO THE BATHROOM... AND I SLEPT FOR A FEW HOURS.

I'VE STUDIED EVERY INCH OF PLASTER ON THIS CEILING.

MY ENTIRE WORLD HAS SHRUNK TO THE SIZE OF THIS ROOM!!

HI, HONEY! — HOW WAS YOUR DAY?!!

IT FEELS WEIRD TO LIE HERE ALL DAY WHILE YOU GO TO WORK.

IT DOES?

WHAT IF I COULDN'T WORK AGAIN? WHAT IF I WAS BEDRIDDEN PERMANENTLY? ...WHAT IF YOU COULDN'T STAND IT AND LEFT ME FOR SOMEBODY ELSE?!!!

HONESTLY JOHN — WHAT'S MAKING YOU THINK SUCH AWFUL THOUGHTS?

I'VE BEEN COOPED UP IN THE HOUSE TOO LONG, EL....

— IT'S SOAP OPERA PSYCHOSIS!!

EEAAHHH

ARRGHHH

OOOOHHHH

GEE.....IT'S GREAT TO BE FEELING BETTER!!

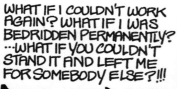

For Better or For Worse

By Lynn Johnston

THIS CLOSET LOOKS STRANGELY BARE. WHERE'S MY STRIPED BLOUSE? WHERE'S MY CARDIGAN? EVEN MY JEANS ARE MISSING!!

ELIZABETH, I FOUND THESE IN YOUR CLOSET!

THOSE ARE YOUR CLOTHES?

SORRY. I'VE HAD THEM FOR SO LONG.... I THOUGHT THEY WERE MINE!!

THAT'S OK, THOUGH — I DON'T MIND IF YOU BORROW THEM!!

— ELIZABETH, WE ARE GOING TO COME TO AN UNDERSTANDING HERE.

YOU DO NOT BORROW MY CLOTHES WITHOUT ASKING. IF YOU WEAR SOMETHING OF MINE, YOU RETURN IT TO ITS PROPER PLACE. NOTHING NEW IS TO BE BORROWED UNTIL THE LAST ITEM IS RETURNED. OK?

OK.

SHE HAS PLENTY TO WEAR, EL. WHY DON'T YOU MAKE YOUR CLOTHES COMPLETELY OFF-LIMITS TO HER?

...SHE LOOKS BETTER IN THEM THAN I DO.

DAWN! IT'S ME! HURRY UP, THE BUS IS COMING!!

KNOCK KNOCK DING DONG

I'M NOT GOING TO SCHOOL, LIZ!!

WHY NOT; ARE YOU SICK? OPEN THE DOOR!

I GOT MY HAIR CUT LAST NIGHT.

YOU'RE NOT GOING TO SCHOOL 'CAUSE OF A HAIR CUT?!!

DON'T BE NUTS, DAWN! — IT COULDN'T BE THAT BAD!!

STUPID ✗◎✳ LOCK !!!

BAM

I HATE CANDACE! — I TOTALLY **HATE** HER !!

RATTLE RATTLE TUG

I HATE HER, I HATE HER !!!

BAM BAM

DAWN!

...**WHO** ARE YOU PUNCHING?

LOOK, WE HAVE A FEW MINUTES, COME ON DOWN TO THE STAFF ROOM.

NOW. WHAT'S HAPPENING?

I (SNIFF) WANTED CANDACE TO LIKE ME. SHE SAID MY HAIR WOULD LOOK GOOD, BUT IT LOOKS AWFUL !!

DAWN.... YOU HAD YOUR HAIR CUT LIKE THAT BECAUSE SOMEONE TOLD YOU TO?

I FEEL LIKE SUCH AN IDIOT !!

I MEAN, I'VE MADE MISTAKES BEFORE... BUT I'VE NEVER HAD TO **WEAR** ONE !!

MISS EDWARDS — I JUST DON'T WANT TO GO TO CLASS LOOKING LIKE THIS !!

THEN DON'T.

EXCUSE ME ?!!

DON'T GO TO CLASS LOOKING LIKE THAT !

PULL UP YOUR COLLAR, PUT A SMILE ON YOUR FACE, LOOK YOUR CRITICS SQUARE IN THE EYE — AND **GO** FOR IT !

I CAN'T.

SURE YOU CAN!

...I'VE BEEN DOING IT FOR **YEARS** !

HI, MOM.

HI, HONEY. WHAT'S NEW?

YOU WON'T BELIEVE WHAT DAWN DID! SHE GOT THE SIDES OF HER HEAD SHAVED 'CAUSE CANDACE TOLD HER TO...AN' SHE IS, LIKE, TOTALLY DIFFERENT!

CANDACE.-ISN'T SHE THE ONE WHO GAVE YOU THE CIGARETTES?

...HOW DID YOU KNOW?

...MOTHERS HAVE A NOSE FOR NICOTINE.

I FOUND THE BUTTS AND THE MATCHES UNDER THE PORCH...AND THE SMELL WAS ON YOUR CLOTHING.

IT'S PRETTY HARD TO HIDE A THING LIKE SMOKING, LIZ.

WE JUST TRIED IT—THAT'S ALL!

IF YOU KNEW WE WERE SMOKING, WHY DIDN'T YOU SAY SOMETHING BEFORE?!!

BECAUSE, UNTIL NOW... I WASN'T REALLY SURE!!

SO...LET'S TALK ABOUT CANDACE, LIZ. SHE TOLD YOU TO SMOKE, RIGHT?

I GUESS.

AND SHE TOLD DAWN TO GET A CRAZY HAIRCUT ...SO SHE DID!

—CANDACE HAS A LOT OF POWER OVER YOU TWO.

NOT!

CANDACE IS JUST...COOL! SHE'S LIKE, YOU KNOW— MORE MATURE!

SHE MAKES YOU THINK SHE KNOWS MORE ABOUT LIFE THAN YOU DO.

YEAH!

ELIZABETH.... THAT'S POWER!!

KNOW WHAT, DAWN? MY MOTHER SAYS CANDACE HAS POWER OVER US. THAT IS SO DUMB. SHE DOESN'T HAVE POWER OVER US!

SHE DID TELL ME TO CUT MY HAIR.

WELL, THAT'S NOT POWER. IF SHE HAD POWER, WE'D, LIKE, BE AFFECTED BY EVERY DUMB THING SHE SAID!

HEY LIZ!!

HEY, NO OFFENSE, BUT YOU SHOULD TRASH THAT SWEATER... IT MAKES YOU LOOK, YOU KNOW... CHUNKY!

CANDACE DID IT TO YOU, LIZ. SHE SAID SOMETHING TO MAKE YOU FEEL LIKE A DWEEB!!

IT'S AMAZING. SHE CAN CHANGE YOUR ENTIRE DAY JUST BY **SAYING** SOMETHING!

DO YOU THINK YOUR MOM'S RIGHT? DO YOU THINK SHE HAS SOME KINDA POWER OVER US?

... ONLY IF YOU **LISTEN.**

HOW COME PEOPLE ARE SO WEIRD TO EACH OTHER, DAWN? I MEAN, WHY DO WE PLAY SO MANY "GAMES"?

LIKE, EVERY TIME YOU MEET SOMEONE, YOU GOTTA FIGURE THEM OUT. YOU CAN'T JUST BE FRIENDS FIRST... YOU GOTTA FIGURE THEM OUT!

AN' SOME PEOPLE YOU CAN NEVER FIGURE OUT-NO MATTER HOW HARD YOU TRY! .... I WONDER WHY SOME PEOPLE ARE SO HARD TO FIGURE OUT.

I DUNNO, LIZ....

... I'M STILL TRYING TO FIGURE OUT **ME** !!!

THEY'RE HERE!!

GRANDMA! GUESS WHAT! - I GOT INTO ADVANCED SKATING, MY CHOIR'S GOING TO OTTAWA, I GOT 90 ON MY LAST MATH TEST, AN'...

HONEY, GRANDMA AND GRANDPA WILL BE HERE FOR 3 WEEKS! - YOU DON'T HAVE TO TELL THEM ALL THE NEWS THE SECOND THEY ARRIVE!!

...SO, WE PUT THE NEW FLOORING IN HERE, AND WE'RE THINKING OF FIXING THE PORCH. JOHN HAS A NEW RECEPTIONIST, THE BABY IS REALLY TALKING NOW, AND...

Lynn

Z

....I SEE YOUR FATHER STILL BELIEVES IN A LONG GRACE.

Lynn

IT'S NICE TO HAVE OUR WHOLE FAMILY TOGETHER - ISN'T IT, PHIL. YES.... IT'S BEEN A WHILE.

WHAT ARE YOU DOING? WATCHING DAD READ TO APRIL. HE USED TO READ TO US LIKE THAT. - REMEMBER?

REMEMBER WHEN HE MADE US THE BIG ROCKING HORSE? - AND THE TIME MOM MADE US ALL MATCHING STRIPED "JAILBIRD" PAJAMAS?

SOME OF THE BEST CHRISTMAS PRESENTS... ARE MEMORIES FROM CHRISTMASES PAST!!

Lynn

NOTE: OBJECTS IN MIRROR MAY BE CLOSER THAN THEY APPEAR!

MMM... SOMETHING SMELLS GOOD IN HERE!

WE'RE DOING SOME CHRISTMAS BAKING.

THIS IS AWESOME!

YEAH! I'M GONNA HAVE ANOTHER PIECE!

GRANDMA-WHY DO THEY (MFF, CRUNCH) CALL THIS "SHORTBREAD"?

... BECAUSE IT DOESN'T LAST **LONG**!!

ELIZABETH, HAVE YOU PACKED FOR YOUR TRIP TO OTTAWA TOMORROW?

UH...NO.

WHY NOT, FOR HEAVEN'S SAKE? YOU'VE HAD ALL EVENING-AND THE BUS GOES AT 7 A.M.!!

TSK!-HERE, LET **ME** DO IT!!

HONESTLY!!IT'S BEYOND ME WHY YOU KIDS ALWAYS LEAVE THESE THINGS 'TIL THE LAST MINUTE!

NOW, I WANT YOU TO DO YOUR HAIR UP WITH THE RED RIBBON, AND MAKE SURE YOUR COLLAR'S PRESSED...

MOM, THE BUS IS LEAVING!

AFTER ALL, IF YOU'RE SINGING ON NATIONAL TELEVISION, YOU SHOULD LOOK YOUR BEST!

MOM!!

THERE ARE 6 CHOIRS!—I'M GONNA BE ONE OF A ZILLION KIDS!—NOBODY'S GONNA NOTICE ME. I'LL JUST BE A TINY LITTLE SPECK!

I KNOW.

....BUT, YOU'LL BE MY TINY LITTLE SPECK.

NIZBEFF ON TV?

SHHHH.... YES, THAT'S ELIZABETH'S CHOIR.

SHH!

TANDO!

MITHMATH!

SHHHHHH YES, THEY ALL HAVE CANDLES.

SHHH-YES IT'S A CHRISTMAS CAROL.

..:SIGH:.. ISN'T THEIR SINGING BEAUTIFUL!

SHHHHHH!!

IT WAS WONDERFUL TO SEE ALL THOSE CHILDREN'S CHOIRS TONIGHT, WASN'T IT, JOHN.

UM-HMMM.

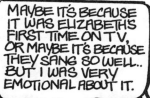

MAYBE IT'S BECAUSE IT WAS ELIZABETH'S FIRST TIME ON T.V., OR MAYBE IT'S BECAUSE THEY SANG SO WELL.. BUT I WAS VERY EMOTIONAL ABOUT IT.

WHEN YOU THINK OF ALL THE TROUBLES IN THE WORLD, IT'S GOOD TO SEE THAT CHILDREN OF ALL NATIONALITIES CAN COME TOGETHER IN PEACE AND HARMONY.

... SHE STARTED IT.

SUDDENLY, THERE WAS THE SOUND OF TINY HOOVES UPON THE ROOF, AND THE DEEP *WHOOSH* OF A HEAVILY LADEN SLEIGH....

A SURPRISE FOR SANTA

SANTA, SLINGING HIS BIG VELVET BAG OVER HIS SHOULDER, STEPPED FROM THE SLEIGH. THEN HE LOOKED DOWN INTO THE RED BRICK CHIMNEY....

WITH A MAGICAL LAUGH, HE DISAPPEARED INTO THE CHIMNEY! DOWN, DOWN HE WENT, CARRYING TOYS AND PRESENTS AND TREATS OF MANY KINDS!!

WOW! CHRISTMAS CAKE!

IT LOOKS LOVELY, DEAR.

NO TANNA?

NO CANDLES ON THIS CAKE, APRIL. THIS ISN'T A BIRTHDAY!!

DUMPY DUMP-DUMP! ♪ DUMPY DUMP-DUMP! FOSTEEEEEE NO MANNN DUMPY DUMP-DUMP!

APRIL LOVES THAT SONG SO MUCH, SHE MUST HAVE PLAYED IT 100 TIMES TODAY! - OVER AND OVER AND OVER AGAIN!

DUMPY DUMP-DUMP!

YOU USED TO DO THAT WHEN YOU WERE LITTLE! IT DIDN'T TAKE LONG BEFORE OUR OLD RECORD PLAYER GAVE UP AND DIED!!

DUMPY DUMP-DUMP!

SIGH... THEY JUST DON'T MAKE THINGS THE WAY THEY USED TO.

DUMPY DUMP-DUMP! DUMPY DUMP-DUMP!

For Better or For Worse
By Lynn Johnston

AH, AH, AH !!!

NO! THAT'S NOT FOR YOU !!

...PUT IT BACK!!

?

THAT'S RIGHT, PUT IT BACK!

NO, YOU MAY NOT BORROW THE CAR, MIKE... UNTIL YOU KICK IN SOME MONEY FOR GAS.

TSK! THERE'S DAD CLEARING THE WALKS. HE SHOULDN'T BE OUT THERE-IT'S MUCH TOO COLD!

NO, I INSIST. YOU COME INSIDE AND PUT YOUR FEET UP!

SIGH!...THEY WON'T LET ME DO ANYTHING!

NO YOU DON'T! THOSE STAIRS CAN SQUEAK FOR A WHILE LONGER!

DAD, YOU'RE NOT HERE TO FIX THINGS! YOU ARE HERE TO ENJOY YOURSELF!!

WHERE ARE YOU GOING? TO TAKE THE DOG FOR A WALK.

...SO AT LEAST ONE OF US CAN GET OFF THE LEASH!!

HERE COMES GRAMPA! HE TOOK THE DOG FOR A WALK!

BACK SO SOON? I WOULD HAVE STAYED OUT LONGER...

BUT AFTER A WHILE, THE COLD GETS TO YOU, THE OLD JOINTS STIFFEN UP AND YOU CAN'T GO ANY FARTHER

...SO I BROUGHT HIM HOME.

DAD—DID YOU GIVE MICHAEL MONEY FOR GAS?

ELLY—IT'S NEW YEAR'S EVE!

YOU CAN'T KEEP A YOUNG MAN HOME WHEN THERE ARE PARTIES TO GO TO, GIRLS TO DANCE WITH... AND THAT MIDNIGHT KISS!!

OK...I GUESS YOU CAN HAVE THE CAR—BUT, ONLY BECAUSE GRANDPA HAS SUCH A GOOD HEART.

....WHAT GRANDPA HAS IS A GOOD MEMORY!

HI, MIKE! HAVE A GOOD TIME AT THE PARTY?

I KNOW IT'S LATE, BUT I WAS AWAKE...SO I THOUGHT I'D GET UP AND WISH YOU HAPPY NEW YEAR!!

GOOD NIGHT, HONEY!

'NIGHT, MOM.

I THINK I JUST PASSED THE "BREATHALYZER KISS"

WELL, WELL...1992 WAS AN EXCITING YEAR—AND IT'S GONE BY ALREADY!

WHAT'S THIS YEAR GOING TO BE LIKE, GRANDMA? WHAT DO YOU THINK IS GOING TO HAPPEN?

I DON'T KNOW.

THAT'S WHAT MAKES THIS NOVEL WE'RE LIVING IN SO INTERESTING, ELIZABETH... YOU CAN'T SKIP A CHAPTER AND LOOK AHEAD!

...YOU HAVE TO FINISH THE PAGES ONE DAY AT A TIME!

THOSE PASSENGERS TRAVELING ON AIR CANADA FLIGHT 407 TO VANCOUVER; YOUR DEPARTURE HAS BEEN DELAYED UNTIL 9:15.

I WISH GRANDMA AND GRANDPA COULD HAVE STAYED LONGER.

ME TOO.

WHY ARE HOLIDAYS ALWAYS OVER SO FAST?

ALREADY WE'VE TAKEN DOWN THE TREE AND ALL THE ORNAMENTS.

THERE'S NOTHING LEFT TO PROVE WE HAD CHRISTMAS AT ALL!!

AAAUGH!

WHAT IS IT, JOHN?

MY BACK! IT'S MY BACK AGAIN!

HOW COULD YOU HURT YOUR BACK? ALL YOU'VE BEEN DOING IS SITTING THERE PAYING THE BILLS!!

WERE YOU CARRYING SOMETHING HEAVY?

...JUST THE WEIGHT OF OUR OVER-DRAFT.

DAD! - YOU'RE WALKING LIKE GRANDMA !!

WHOA! - CHECK OUT THE DAD-MAN! ... DOES THE NAME "QUASIMODO" RING A BELL?

YOU SHOULD REALLY GO AND SEE SOMEONE, JOHN. HONESTLY, IF YOU DON'T START LOOKING AFTER YOURSELF, WHO KNOWS WHAT SORT OF TROUBLE....

...SOMETIMES.... MISERY DOES **NOT** LOVE COMPANY !

HELLO, THE NAME IS JOHN PATTERSON. I HAVE AN APPOINTMENT.

YES. PLEASE HAVE A SEAT, DR. PATTERSON.

RECEPTION

I'VE BEEN HERE FOR OVER HALF AN HOUR! .... HOW MUCH LONGER IS HE GOING TO BE?

ONE THING A DOCTOR HATES IS TO BE KEPT WAITING !!!

DR. PATTERSON? WHAT SEEMS TO BE THE PROBLEM?

I PUT MY BACK OUT.

L. LAYCOCK CHIROPRACTO

ACTUALLY, THERE'S NO SUCH THING AS "PUTTING ONE'S BACK OUT." WHAT YOU'VE DONE IS PUT STRESS ON SOME MUSCLE, HERE !!

PEOPLE ALWAYS SAY THEY PUT THEIR BACK OUT, BUT IT'S NOT POSSIBLE TO "PUT YOUR BACK OUT" — SO.... HEH, HEH.... LET ME SET YOU STRAIGHT !

SET YOU STRAIGHT !! - GET IT ?!!

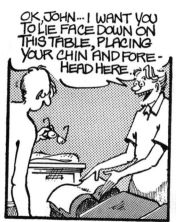

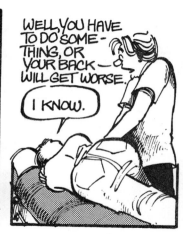

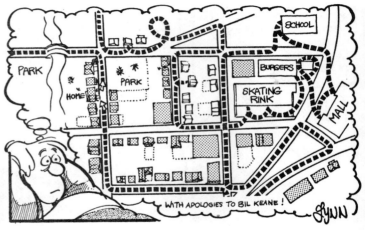

WITH APOLOGIES TO BIL KEANE!

86

I MISSED THE EXIT! I MISSED THE *ø EXIT! IT WASN'T MARKED! I WASN'T READY!

OK, OK, I'LL GET OFF AT WAVERLEY ST. NORTH.. IT SHOULD TAKE ME BACK TO HWY. 16.

WAIT A MINUTE! THIS LOOKS LIKE THE MUNICIPAL AIRPORT! HWY. 16 IS SOUTH OF HERE! I HAFTA GO SOUTH! .. OK,- I'LL GO RIGHT AT THE NEXT STREET AN' THEN RIGHT AGAIN.

....TROUBLE WITH ROAD MAPS IS ... THEY'RE HARD TO READ THROUGH TEARS.

NO EXIT

NO TRESPASS

WHERE IS HE? WHEN THAT KID COMES HOME, BELIEVE ME, THERE IS GOING TO BE TROUBLE!!

I KNEW I SHOULDN'T HAVE GIVEN HIM THAT CAR... ONCE HE GOT BEHIND THE WHEEL, I KNEW SOMETHING WOULD HAPPEN!

THEN WHY DID YOU LET HIM GO?

WELL...

—YOU CAN SAY YOU KNOW SOMETHING WILL HAPPEN .... BUT YOU ALWAYS HOPE THAT IT WON'T!

HONEY, MICHAEL'S USUALLY HOME ON TIME. MAYBE SOMETHING'S WRONG!

SOMETHING'S WRONG, ALL RIGHT. - I LENT HIM MY CAR!

... MAYBE SOMETHING HAPPENED, AND HE CAN'T GET HOME!!

SNARL.. GRUMBLE

INSTEAD OF BEING MAD, MAYBE WE SHOULD BE WORRIED!

ELLY, IF THERE WAS SOMETHING WRONG, HE WOULD HAVE CALLED!

SORRY, THIS PHONE'S FOR PRIVATE USE. THERE'S A PAY PHONE TWO MILES BACK.

GREAT! THE FIRST TIME DAD LENDS ME HIS CAR, AND I HAVE TO GET TOTALLY LOST!!

I SHOULD HAVE BEEN BACK HALF AN HOUR AGO. HE IS GONNA **KILL** ME!!

PLEEASE, PLEEASE..... I'M DESPERATE! THERE'S ONLY ONE PERSON WHO CAN SAVE MY BUTT ON THIS ONE!

CHING!

.....HELLO? **MOM**?!!

WELL, MICHAEL...IT'S ABOUT TIME.

I'M SORRY, DAD, I...

YOU TOOK MY CAR FOR WHAT SHOULD HAVE BEEN A 40-MINUTE ROUND-TRIP... BUT YOU WENT OUT ON THE FREEWAY, AND CAME BACK ALMOST AN HOUR LATE!!!

WAIT, HONEY. HE DIDN'T MEAN..

YOU'RE IN SOME TROUBLE, MIKE. WHAT DO YOU HAVE TO SAY FOR YOUR-SELF?

— I'D LIKE TO INTRODUCE MY COUNSEL FOR THE DEFENSE!

HE DIDN'T MEAN TO GET LOST, HONEY.

HE SHOULDN'T HAVE BEEN ON THE FREEWAY IN THE FIRST PLACE!

—I SAID TO COME STRAIGHT HOME!

THE FREEWAY IS A ROUTE HOME.

HE KNOWS IT'S FASTER TO COME HOME BY MAIN AND BECKER!

YOU DIDN'T TELL HIM TO COME HOME BY MAIN AND BECKER!

ELLY, HE'S ALMOST AN ADULT!!—DO I HAVE TO TELL HIM **EVERY-THING**?!!

RHETORICAL QUESTION - OBVIOUSLY ANSWERED "YES" —THE ATTORNEY FOR THE DEFENSE SCORES ANOTHER POINT!

SO ... WHAT'D YOU GET?

A DRIVING SUSPENSION FOR ONE WEEK AND AN "INDEFINITE" BAN ON THE SPORTS CAR

I'M PROUD OF US, EL. WE CAME TO A DECISION LAST NIGHT, WE TOLD MICHAEL WHAT THE VERDICT WAS, AND WE STUCK TO IT!

DISCIPLINING SOMEONE YOU LOVE IS NEVER EASY... BUT IT HAS TO BE DONE QUICKLY, FAIRLY AND WITHOUT GUILT.

WHAT ARE YOU DOING?

... MAKING HIM A NICE LUNCH.

SHE SWALLOWED THE CAT TO CATCH THE BIRD, SHE SWALLOWED THE BIRD TO CATCH THE SPIDER - THAT WRIGGLED AND WRIGGLED AND TICKLED INSIDE HER.... SHE SWALLOWED THE SPIDER TO CATCH THE FLY - BUT, I DON'T KNOW WHY SHE SWALLOWED THE FLY....

COME ON, APRIL-TIME FOR BREAKFAST!

APRIL!

WHY DON'T YOU JUST SAY YOU'RE NOT HUNGRY?!!

CRUNCH CHOMP SLURP

APRIL HAS YOU WRAPPED AROUND HER LITTLE FINGER, JOHN.

I THOUGHT YOU WERE TOO STRICT, EL.

I WAS, FAIR!

BUT SHE'S SO LITTLE!

WHAT'S HAPPENING? WE'RE SUPPOSED TO BE TOGETHER IN OUR DISCIPLINE! WHERE'S THE FIRM SUPPORT? WHAT HAPPENED TO OUR UNITED FRONT ?!!

... I THINK IT LIFTED AND SEPARATED.

IT'S HARD TO KNOW HOW TO HANDLE BEHAVIOR PROBLEMS SOMETIMES, JOHN....

SO OFTEN, WHEN THERE'S A CONFRONTATION...ONE OF US IS TOUGH, AND ONE OF US IS A MARSHMALLOW!

THE HARDEST PART OF RAISING KIDS IS DISCIPLINING THEM— AND THERE ARE **TWO** OF US! .... HOW ON EARTH DO SINGLE PARENTS MANAGE ?!!

I DON'T KNOW, EL.

.... I GUESS THERE ARE A LOT OF TOUGH MARSHMALLOWS OUT THERE !!

Z

YAWNNN SMACK-SMACK

SHAKE, SHAKE

SHAKE SHAKE

94

APRIL! THOSE ARE MY CLOTHES!! - WHY DON'T YOU PULL ALL THE STUFF OUT OF YOUR OWN DRAWERS?

...'CAUSE I KNOW WHAT'S IN DEM!!

YOU'RE LUCKY, DAWN. YOU DON'T HAFTA SHARE YOUR ROOM WITH SOME BRAT OF A LITTLE SISTER!

APRIL IS, LIKE, TOTALLY INTO EVERYTHING! - IF I LEAVE SOMETHING ON THE FLOOR, SHE GETS IT. IF I PUT SOMETHING DOWN...IT'S GONE!

JUST TO KEEP HER OUT OF MY STUFF, I HAFTA KEEP MY ROOM TIDY ALL THE TIME!!

BUMMER.

BIG TIME.

STTTT

MOM, YOU JUST GOTTA DO SOMETHING ABOUT APRIL! - SHE GETS INTO EVERYTHING I OWN!

SHE OPENS MY DRAWERS, SHE TEARS MY BOOKS. - I DON'T WANNA SHARE A ROOM WITH HER. - IT'S NOT FAIR!!

I KNOW, LIZ.

AS A MATTER OF FACT, WE'RE PLANNING TO PUT A SMALL ADDITION ONTO THE HOUSE SO THAT YOU CAN HAVE A ROOM OF YOUR OWN.

OH, COOL!!

WON'T THAT BE EXPENSIVE?

SURE.... BUT THE COST OF COMPROMISE IS ALWAYS LESS THAN THE COST OF WAR.

WOW! WHAT'S THIS? THESE ARE BUILDING PLANS FOR AN ADDITION TO THE HOUSE.

GRANDMA GAVE US SOME MONEY FOR CHRISTMAS. YOUR DAD AND I THOUGHT THIS WOULD BE THE BEST WAY TO USE IT.

WE WILL BE MOVING DOWNSTAIRS, SO YOU WILL EACH HAVE YOUR OWN BEDROOM. ...THIS WAY, THERE'LL BE NO MORE ARGUMENTS.

....AND IF THERE ARE WE WON'T BE ABLE TO HEAR THEM!

HERE WE ARE, PUTTING AN ADDITION ONTO THE HOUSE.—WE'RE REALLY GOING TO DO IT!

ELIZABETH SHOULD HAVE HER OWN ROOM, JOHN. SHE'S A YOUNG WOMAN NOW. SHE NEEDS HER PRIVACY.

YES. I CAN'T BELIEVE HOW MUCH SHE'S CHANGED!

MICHAEL TOO. ....IT WON'T BE LONG BEFORE THEY'RE BOTH GROWN UP AND MOVED AWAY!

....AND HERE WE ARE PUTTING AN ADDITION ONTO THE HOUSE !!!

PIZZA DAY! DON'T FORGET IT'S PIZZA DAY! SUPPORT THE VOLLEYBALL TEAM, AN' BRING YOUR MONEY TO ROOM 212! — IT'S PIZZA DAY!!

YOU GONNA GO FOR IT, LIZ? NAH. I WENT FOR IT LAST TIME.

BUT THE LAST TIME WAS 4 WEEKS AGO! —HOW COME YOU DON'T WANNA GET PIZZA TODAY?

....I'VE STILL GOT SOME LEFT.

For Better or For Worse
By Lynn Johnston

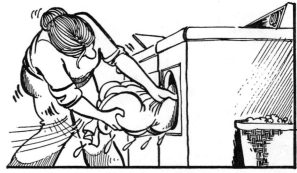

WHRRR RRRr

WHRRRRRRR

DING!

AAAAGH!! THERE'S MELTED LIPSTICK ALL OVER THE LAUNDRY!!!

ELIZABETH?

I KNOW. I'M SORRY. IT'S MY FAULT.

...I'VE BEEN WEARING LIPSTICK AT SCHOOL.

BUT WHY DO YOU KEEP IT IN YOUR POCKET?

...I DIDN'T WANT YOU TO KNOW!

YOUR HAIR HAS REALLY GROWN BACK, DAWN!

YEAH. I LIKE IT NOW.

YOU WOULDN'T THINK THAT HAIR WAS SO IMPORTANT - BUT IT IS! IF YOUR HAIR ISN'T RIGHT, THEN, LIKE, NOTHING IS RIGHT!

I MEAN, YOUR HAIR IS PART OF YOUR PERSONALITY. THE WAY YOU WEAR IT, LIKE, SAYS WHERE YOUR HEAD IS AT!

....OR MAYBE NOT.

...TINK!

UH, DUANE, YOU DROPPED THIS

THANKS, MAN.

I GOT MY NOSE PIERCED, AN' LIKE, THIS THING DOESN'T WANNA STAY IN.

IN THIS SENTENCE, THE VERB "SEEN" HAS BEEN USED INCORRECTLY. "I SEEN" IS INCORRECT. THE WORD WE WANT HERE IS "SAW".

OK! I GOT IT! SAW!!! -LIKE, SAY YOU HAD A SAW, RIGHT? YOU CAN'T, LIKE, SAY YOU SEEN THE SAW-SO, CAN YOU SAY YOU HAVE SAW THE SAW?!!

YOU CAN'T SAW THE SAW, MAN!

I SEEN SOMEONE SAW!

THERE WAS A SAW IN A SCENE I SAW!

SEE?

SO?

...I LOVE IT WHEN WE HAVE A SUB!

I see
I saw
I have see
I will see

CANDACE, CAN WE, UM.... TALK TO YOU FOR A MINUTE?

I GUESS.

MAYBE YOU'RE ASKING FOR TROUBLE-WEARING CLOTHES LIKE THAT TO SCHOOL.

WHAT?!! THIS IS A DESIGNER OUTFIT!!

THIS BLOUSE WAS OVER $100 AND THE SKIRT WAS $150! WITH THE BOOTS AN' EVERYTHING, I BET THIS IS WORTH OVER $350!

WOW! -- I NEVER KNEW HOW EXPENSIVE IT IS TO LOOK CHEAP!!

I DON'T UNDERSTAND CANDACE, LIZ.

OR DUANE EITHER!

I MEAN, THEY DON'T LIKE IT IF YOU STARE AT THEM, BUT THEY'RE ALWAYS DOING STUFF THAT MAKES YOU STARE AT THEM!!

I DUNNO, DAWN...WHAT IF WE'RE THE ONES WHO ARE WEIRD! MAYBE THEY WALK AROUND ALL DAY, WONDERING ABOUT US!!

SCARY, ISN'T IT.

TOTALLY.

For Better or For Worse

By Lynn Johnston

THIS WAS A GREAT IDEA, EL. WE HAVEN'T HAD LUNCH TOGETHER FOR AGES!

I KNOW!

I HAD NO IDEA HOW BUSY I'D BE WITH 3 KIDS, CONNIE! THERE'S SO MUCH GOING ON, I CAN'T REMEMBER WHEN WE'VE HAD AN EVENING OR A WEEKEND FREE!

MY PROBLEM IS THAT OUR KIDS ARE ALL SO GROWN UP AND INDEPENDENT, THEY'RE NEVER HOME!!

THAT'S A PROBLEM?!!

WHEN GREG'S GIRLS MOVED IN WITH US, I THOUGHT I'D GO CRAZY. ....I MISS THEM NOW.

MOLLY'S IN COLLEGE, AND GAYLE'S GONE TO STAY WITH HER MOM. – LAWRENCE IS NEVER HOME. THINGS ARE PRETTY QUIET FOR ME, EL.

SO. NOW'S THE TIME TO FOCUS ON **YOU**! FIX UP THE HOUSE, PUT IN GOOD CARPET, GET THAT NEW FURNITURE YOU'VE ALWAYS WANTED!!

WHAT'S THE POINT IN FEATHERING A NEST.... WHEN IT'S EMPTY!!?

YOU MAY WANT FREEDOM AND PEACE AND QUIET NOW, EL-BUT WHEN THE KIDS ARE ALL GONE...IT'S A REAL ADJUSTMENT.

BUT, CONNIE, YOU HAVE SO MANY INTERESTS! WHAT ABOUT TRAVEL? START A NEW HOBBY! GO BACK TO SCHOOL!

I'M TELLING YOU – WHEN MY KIDS ARE ON THEIR OWN, I'M GOING TO DO ALL THE THINGS I CAN'T DO NOW.

LIKE?

.... HAVE A BATH UNINTERRUPTED.

KNOW WHAT I'M LOOKING FORWARD TO, EL? GRANDCHILDREN!

GRANDCHILDREN?

YOU'LL HAVE A LONG WAIT, CONNIE. GREG'S GIRLS BOTH WANT CAREERS FIRST AND LAWRENCE IS ONLY 17.

I KNOW.

BUT I WANT A BABY TO HOLD IN MY ARMS! I WANT A LITTLE ONE TO TAKE CARE OF! HOW CAN ONE CURB THESE INSTINCTS?

© 1993 Lynn Johnston

... BORROW MINE!

Lynn

LET'S GO IN HERE, CONNIE ... I WANT TO BUY ANOTHER RUBBER POSTMAN.

RUBBER POSTMAN?

PET OWN

FARLEY GOES THROUGH ONE OF THESE A MONTH!

THEY DON'T MAKE RUBBER POSTMEN LIKE THEY USED TO!

BACK TO OUR DISCUSSION ABOUT BABIES, CONNIE... I THINK YOU'RE JUST GOING THROUGH A PHASE. YOU DON'T REALLY WANT ANOTHER BABY, YOU JUST....

PET SUPPLIES

FLEA SHAMPOO

CONNIE?!!

Lynn

ELLY, ISN'T SHE THE MOST ADORABLE PUPPY YOU EVER SAW?!!

CONNIE, YOU DON'T WANT A PUPPY!

I'M NOT GOING TO BUY A DOG, EL! ..... DO YOU THINK THEY'D LET ME HOLD HER IF I ASKED?

DON'T LOOK AT ME LIKE THAT! I JUST WANT TO PICK HER UP!—THE LAST THING I NEED IS A PUPPY!!!

..... HOW MUCH?

Lynn

CONNIE BOUGHT A PUPPY TODAY, JOHN.

THAT'S NICE.

YOU DON'T UNDERSTAND! —SHE DOESN'T REALLY WANT A DOG. SHE WANTS ANOTHER BABY!!—SHE BOUGHT IT AS A CHILD SUBSTITUTE!

WHAM!

....SENSIBLE MOVE.

JOHN, YOU DON'T JUST GO OUT AND BUY A PUPPY WITHOUT TALKING IT OVER WITH YOUR FAMILY FIRST!—THIS IS A MAJOR DECISION!

WHAT'S GREG GOING TO SAY WHEN HE COMES HOME AND FINDS A CAGE IN THE HALLWAY?!!

YIP?

SO, YOU WON'T BELIEVE IT... I COME HOME, AN' I HEAR THIS SOUND, RIGHT?

I GO THROUGH THE KITCHEN, AN' THERE IN THE HALL IS A CAGE WITH THIS PUPPY IN IT!!—MY MOTHER BOUGHT A DOG!

ALL MY LIFE, I BEGGED FOR A DOG, GUYS-AN' NOW THAT I'M ALMOST OUT OF HIGH SCHOOL—BINGO! GO FIGURE!...IS SHE NUTS?

ALL PARENTS ARE NUTS, LAWRENCE. IT'S NOT 'TIL YOU'RE OUR AGE THAT IT'S NOTICEABLE!

WHAT'S HER NAME?

WE HAVEN'T DECIDED YET.

WHAT KIND OF DOG IS SHE? PART COLLIE? PART AIREDALE? PART LAB?

WE'RE NOT SURE!

...BUT SHE SEEMS TO BE **ALL** LOVE!!

AN' IT'S NOT JUST MY MOM WHO'S CRAZY ABOUT HER... MY STEPFATHER'S GONE NUTS ABOUT HER, TOO!

WHERE'S THE BABY?

OOHH... IS SHE OUR GOOD GIRL? - IS SHE THE CUTEST PUPPY ON EARTH? YES SHE IS!!

THEY'VE WIGGED, GUYS! - WHAT DO YOU DO WHEN BOTH YOUR PARENTS TOTALLY LOSE THEIR SANITY?

- I'D ASK FOR A RAISE IN MY ALLOWANCE.

SHE'S DOING SO WELL, ELLY! SHE WAS ONLY UP TWICE DURING THE NIGHT!

SHE MESSED ON THE HALL FLOOR AND CHEWED THE COFFEE TABLE... BUT THESE THINGS HAPPEN!

MOM - YOU NEVER LET ME GET AWAY WITH STUFF LIKE THAT!

BECAUSE YOU WERE MY FIRST CHILD, HONEY!

...PARENTS ARE ALWAYS MORE LENIENT WITH THE SECOND!!

For Better or For Worse

By Lynn Johnston

GOOD. I SEE MIKE BATHED THE DOG LIKE I ASKED HIM TO!!

SNIFFFFFFF...AAHHHH WHAT A BEAUTIFUL CRISP SPRING DAY!

ON DAYS LIKE THIS, MY MOM WOULD HANG ALL OUR LAUNDRY OUTSIDE AND LET IT BLOW IN THE WIND.

I REMEMBER THE SQUEAK OF THE CLOTHESLINE, AND THE SMELL OF FRESH, CLEAN SHEETS!...THOSE WERE THE DAYS!!

NOW WHEN PEOPLE AIR THEIR LAUNDRY OUT IN THE OPEN....IT'S ON OPRAH!

'BYE, MOM!-I'M TAKING APRIL NEXT DOOR TO SEE THE NEW PUPPY!

HAVE YOU THOUGHT OF A NAME FOR HER YET, LAWRENCE?

MOM LIKES "SERENDIPITY."

WHAT?!!

'CAUSE SHE WAS A SPUR-OF-THE-MOMENT THING. YOU KNOW! - SHE'D PROBABLY BE "SARA" FOR SHORT.

.....OR MAYBE DIPPITY!!

YAP YIP YAP!

SARA IS A DUMB NAME FOR A DOG, MAN.

SHE SHOULD BE TRIXIE OR LADY OR MAX!

MAX?

FOR MAXINE!-OR HARRIET -YOU COULD CALL HER "HAIRY" FOR SHORT!

HOW 'BOUT LUCKY OR CASEY OR BUTTONS OR....

ACTUALLY, IT DOESN'T REALLY MATTER WHAT YOU CALL A DOG, GUYS.

YEAH...

- OURS ONLY COMES IF YOU YELL "FOOD"!!

SHRIEK! GIGGLE GIGGLE GIGGLE!

GIGGLE GIGGLE GIGGLE!

RRRR

GIGGLE GIGGLE (GASP!) GIGGLE GIGGLE

YAP! YAP! YAP!

WE THOUGHT YOUR PUPPY WOULD LIKE TO PLAY WITH SOMEONE HER OWN AGE!

GIGGLE GIGGLE GIGGLE!

Lynn

I CAN'T GET OVER HOW MUCH MY MOM LOVES THAT DOG, MAN.

YEAH.

KNOW WHAT SHE TOLD MY MOM? SHE SAID THE PUPPY WOULD KEEP HER HAPPY 'TIL YOU HAD CHILDREN!

WHAT?

THEN THAT PUPPY BETTER LIVE A LONG TIME, MIKE, BECAUSE I'M PROBABLY NEVER GONNA HAVE CHILDREN.

HEY, HOW DO YOU KNOW?

..'CAUSE I'M PROBABLY NEVER GOING TO GET MARRIED.

EVER.

Lynn

WHAT DO YOU MEAN, YOU'RE NEVER GOING TO GET MARRIED?!

I'M JUST NOT, MIKE.

IT'S NOT A DECISION I'VE CONSCIOUSLY MADE... IT'S JUST THE WAY I AM.

I DON'T GET WHAT YOU'RE SAYING, MAN! WHAT IF YOU, YOU KNOW-FALL IN LOVE?

I HAVE FALLEN IN LOVE.

...BUT IT'S NOT WITH A GIRL.

Lynn

ARE YOU OK?

YEAH. I'M OK NOW.

LAWRENCE, WHAT I WANNA KNOW IS—WHEN?

...I'VE KNOWN I WAS DIFFERENT FOR A COUPLE OF YEARS. BUT IT WAS ALWAYS THERE.

IT'S KIND OF INTERESTING, MIKE! THE ABORIGINAL PEOPLE CONSIDERED US "MYSTICS". THEY CALL US "TWO SPIRITED"—MEANING THAT WE'RE BLESSED WITH BOTH MALE AND FEMALE SPIRITS!!

LIKE, HALF OF YOU WANTS TO SHOP—AND THE OTHER HALF WANTS TO WATCH FOOTBALL?!

SO. TELL ME ABOUT THIS, ...UM.... PERSON.

HIS NAME IS BEN. I MET HIM SKIING!

HE IS SO NEAT, MIKE! HE PLAYS THE PIANO, HE SINGS...HE WANTS TO BE A PHARMACIST!

WOW!—BEING HONEST WITH YOU IS SUCH A RELIEF!!

..DOES THIS MEAN YOU'RE "OUT OF THE CLOSET"?

NO...I'VE JUST OPENED THE DOOR ENOUGH SO I CAN SEE OUTSIDE.

MICHAEL.... I WANNA KNOW HOW YOU FEEL ABOUT ME.

I DON'T KNOW HOW I FEEL, MAN.

ALL I KNOW IS..EVERYTHING'S DIFFERENT. IT'S NEVER GOING TO BE THE SAME, LAWRENCE. WE'LL ALWAYS KNOW EACH OTHER... ...BUT, IT WILL NEVER BE THE SAME.

SLUG!

WE'VE NARROWED DOWN THE NAMES FOR CONNIE'S PUPPY, MIKE! IT'S TAWNY OR AMBER OR....

YOU'RE NOT LISTENING TO ME.

HOW DO YOU KNOW I'M NOT LISTENING TO YOU?

YOU'VE GOT THAT "LOOK."

WHAT "LOOK"?

LIKE, WHEN MOM OR DAD IS LECTURING YOU.

WHAT'S THAT?

IT'S A DIARY.

YOU'RE WRITING IN A DIARY? GET OUT!!—MY BROTHER KEEPS A DIARY! —LEMME SEE!

IT'S PRIVATE, OK? BACK OFF!!

THIS IS SO AMAZING!—I NEVER THOUGHT THAT A GUY WOULD....

WHAT MAKES YOU THINK IT'S ONLY GIRLS WHO KEEP DIARIES?!!

...IT'S A SIGN OF INTELLIGENCE.

SO, WHAT IF I FOUND YOUR DIARY SOMETIME—AN' READ ALL YOUR SECRET STUFF?!

YOU WOULDN'T DO THAT.

YOU ARE SO TOTALLY SERIOUS, MIKE!—WHAT'S BUGGING YOU?

I CAN'T TELL YOU, LIZ. I CAN'T TELL ANYONE.

SO, WHAT'S THE POINT IN TELLING STUFF TO A DIARY? —IT DOESN'T HAVE ANY ANSWERS!

I KNOW...

—BUT IT HELPS ME UNDERSTAND THE QUESTIONS.

SO, WHAT ARE YOU GOING TO CALL THIS PUPPY, CONNIE?

I DON'T KNOW, EL. NOTHING SEEMS TO FIT.

BARLEY'S TOO CLOSE TO FARLEY... MILLIE'S TOO FAMOUS... I WANT SOMETHING UNIQUE! SOMETHING NOBODY ELSE HAS THOUGHT OF!

WHY DON'T YOU CALL IT SARA? YOU KNOW, FOR "SERENDIPITY"- LIKE YOU FIRST WANTED TO!

- OR YOU COULD JUST CALL IT QUITS!!

SHE HAS TO KNOW, LAWRENCE.

I CAN'T, MIKE.

WHAT DO I DO? TELL MY MOTHER I'M GAY? JUST LIKE THAT?

NO! TELL HER THE TRUTH! THE WAY YOU TOLD ME!

- AND, DO IT SOON!

I'M AFRAID TO.

IT WILL BE A SHOCK IF I TELL HER!

IT WILL BE A LIE IF YOU DON'T.

YOU'RE AWFULLY QUIET, LAWRENCE.

MOM... THERE'S SOMETHING I HAVE TO TELL YOU.

WELL, IF IT'S ABOUT THE MISSING TOOLBOX, WE FOUND IT- AND DON'T WORRY ABOUT THE SCRATCH ON THE CAR...

-IT'S NOT ABOUT THAT-IT'S ABOUT ME!

THIS ISN'T GOING TO BE EASY.

DON'T WORRY, HONEY. WHATEVER IT IS, WE'LL HANDLE IT TOGETHER-CALMLY AND SENSIBLY.

I'M GAY.

DON'T BE RIDICULOUS!

RINGG!!

SNORK...SNOGG... UH? HELLO?

CONNIE? IT'S 2 A.M.!!

I'M SORRY, EL! GREG MADE LAWRENCE LEAVE THE HOUSE! I CAN'T STAND IT ANY LONGER! IS HE THERE?!

UH? (SNOGG...ZZZ)...I DUNNO. I DON'T THINK SO, BUT I'LL CHECK.

—HANG ON.

CLONGK!

LYNN

WAKE UP, HONEY... LAWRENCE IS MISSING!

UH? WHAT?

MISSING? I DON'T UNDERSTAND!

APPARENTLY HE SAID SOMETHING — AND GREG THREW HIM OUT OF THE HOUSE!

CONNIE IS READY TO CALL THE HOSPITALS AND THE POLICE.

...GREG FEELS AWFUL!

STRANGE... AND THEY ACCUSE **US** OF ACTING FIRST AND THINKING AFTERWARD!

LYNN

I LET MIKE HAVE THE CAR, CONNIE. HE THINKS HE KNOWS WHERE LAWRENCE IS.

TELL HIM TO BE CAREFUL.

LAWRENCE HAS BEEN ACTING... STRANGELY. — WHO KNOWS WHAT SORT OF PLACE HE'S GONE...OR WHAT KIND OF PEOPLE HE'S WITH!

24 HOUR COFFEE & DONUTS

SANDWICH
HAMBURG
HOT DOG

LYNN

HI.

OH. HI.

I'M SORRY THIS HAPPENED TO YOU, LAWRENCE.

YEAH? WELL, I'M NOT THE FIRST GAY PERSON TO BE THROWN OUT ONTO THE STREET ...AND I WON'T BE THE LAST.

AND I DON'T NEED ANYONE TO FEEL SORRY FOR ME, OK?

FINE.

...IS IT OK IF I FEEL ANGRY FOR YOU?

WHAT ARE YOU DOING HERE, MIKE?

I JUST THOUGHT I'D SHOW UP.

IT'S 3 A.M. GO HOME TO BED.

AND LEAVE YOU HERE?... I DON'T THINK SO.

LEAVE ME ALONE, OK? YOU CAN'T HELP ME—I'M SICK!

YOU'RE NOT SICK, MAN! TRUST ME!—I'M MORE OPEN-MINDED THAN YOU THINK!!

BELIEVE ME! AFTER 11 JELLY DONUTS AND 6 COFFEES, —I'M SICK!!

COME ON. LET'S GO OUT-SIDE. THE AIR WILL DO YOU GOOD.

LOOK. THE SUN'S UP ALREADY.

YEAH.

THAT MEANS I'VE BEEN OFFICIALLY OUTCAST FOR 9 HOURS AND 32 MINUTES EXACTLY.

IT ALSO MEANS IT'S THE START OF A WHOLE NEW DAY.

I CALLED YOUR MOM. SHE'S WAITING FOR US. LET'S GO HOME, OK?

MIKE... REMEMBER WHEN YOU SAID THAT NOTHING WOULD EVER BE THE SAME BETWEEN US.... THAT WE'D PROBABLY ALWAYS KNOW EACH OTHER - BUT THAT'S ALL?

YES.

.... I'M GLAD I KNOW YOU.

I DON'T THINK I'LL EVER UNDERSTAND, LAWRENCE. BUT I'LL TRY. I'LL DO MY BEST TO ACCEPT YOUR LIFESTYLE... AND YOUR FRIENDS.

YOUR MOTHER HAS KNOWN YOU AND LOVED YOU FOR 17 YEARS. I'VE JUST BEEN A SMALL PART OF YOUR LIFE. - I'M NOT GOING TO JUDGE YOU.

AS LONG AS YOU'RE A GOOD MAN.... AND A KIND MAN - I'LL RESPECT YOU.

... AS FOR THE REST.. WHAT WILL BE WILL BE. QUE SERA SERA.

NOW I KNOW FOR SURE. ... I'M CALLING YOU "SERA"

SNORK **BAM!**

BAM! BAM, BAM...WHACK! BAM, BAM!

WA'S THAT?

I DUNNO... MUS' BE THE CONSTRUCTION CREW.

THEY SAID THEY'D BE HERE SOMETIME THIS WEEK.

WHY DIDN'T YOU TELL ME?

I FIGURED THAT "SOMETIME THIS WEEK" MEANT *FRIDAY!!*

'ALLO, MADAME! — I AM PAUL GAUTHIER, YOUR CONTRACTEUR....

WE ARE STARTING YOUR RENOVATION.

BUT... IT'S 7 O'CLOCK IN THE MORNING!!

MY APOLOGIES, MADAME!

TOMORROW, WE WILL TRY TO BE HERE EARLIER!

BAM, BAM...WHACKK...BANG...BAM, BAN! CRACK, BAM!

WHAT'S GOING ON?

THE CARPENTERS HAVE STARTED WORKING ON OUR HOUSE.

OH, MAN—I'M GONNA MISS MY BUS!—SEE YA!

WAIT!

WATCH OUT FOR THE BACK PORCH!

WHY?

...IT'S GONE.

WE'RE FINALLY ADDING THAT EXTRA BEDROOM, ANNE! THEY STARTED TODAY!

I KNOW... AT 7 AM.

IT'S A MAJOR RENOVATION - BUT AT LEAST THE KIDS WILL EACH HAVE A ROOM OF THEIR OWN.

THAT'S SOMETHING I'VE ALWAYS DREAMED OF, EL.

WHAT? - AN EXTRA BEDROOM FOR THE KIDS?

NO .... A ROOM OF MY OWN !!

AND IF YOU'VE GOT SOMETHING THAT MUST BE DONE, BUT IT CAN ONLY BE DONE BY ONE THEN, THERE IS NOTHING MORE TO SAAAAYYY...

EXCEPT IT'S A LOVELY DAY FOR SAYINGGG IT'S A LOVELY DAAYY!

THAT WAS ARNOLD ROTH AND THE CLAMDIP TRIO PLAYING "IT'S A LOVELY DAY"!

HAH! - I WONDER HOW MANY OF OUR LISTENERS ARE OLD ENOUGH TO REMEMBER **THAT** ONE !!

YOU'RE IN A GOOD MOOD TODAY, EL!

I KNOW! - THE CARPENTERS ARRIVED THIS MORNING. THEY'VE STARTED WORKING ON THE NEW BEDROOM!

WE ARE MOVING DOWNSTAIRS TO COMPLETE PRIVACY! - FULL BATH, WALK-IN CLOSET AND ROOM FOR A QUEEN-SIZED BED !!

...SOUNDS EXPENSIVE.

YEAH .... BUT WE DECIDED - WHAT THE HECK ! ... IT'S FOR THE KIDS !

JOHN, WHAT AM I GOING TO DO WITH-OUT ANNIE? APRIL'S NEVER BEEN IN A DAYCARE CENTER!

WELL, MAYBE IT'S TIME, EL! - APRIL SHOULD BE WITH PEOPLE HER OWN AGE!

BESIDES - SHE NEEDS AN ENVIRONMENT WHERE SHE CAN LEARN NEW THINGS! ... ARTS AND CRAFTS, FOR EXAMPLE.

YOU THINK SO?

SURE! - WHO KNOWS... MAYBE SHE HAS SOME REAL ARTISTIC TALENT!!

BZZZZANGGGG... BAM, BAM, BANG, BANG, WHAK, BANG!

BAM   BAM BANG!

DAIRIES, DANCE, DATA, DATING ..... DAY CARE!

BANG BANG BAM!

6 WEEKS? - IS THERE ANY WAY I COULD BRING HER IN SOONER?

BAM BAM BANG BAM WHACK!

SOMETHING WRONG, MOM?

...I HAVE A POUND-ING HEADACHE!

BAM BAM BA WH BA

GOOD NEWS, ANNE! I FOUND A DAY CARE CENTER THAT CAN TAKE APRIL NEXT WEEK!

WE GO IN FOR TWO MORNINGS SO SHE CAN MEET EVERYONE - AND THEN WE'LL TRY HER ON HER OWN!

ELLY, I....

LOOK, DON'T FEEL GUILTY ABOUT TAKING THIS JOB. YOU NEED THE CHANGE, YOU NEED TO GET OUT...

I NEED THE MONEY.

FRIENDS!!

HOW DID THE INTRODUCTION TO DAY CARE GO, EL?

FINE! APRIL HAS A FRIEND ALREADY.

I THINK THIS WAS A GOOD THING, ANNIE. APRIL DOES NEED TO BE WITH OTHER CHILDREN.

AFTER ALL, IT WON'T BE LONG BEFORE SHE'S IN KINDERGARTEN... AND GRADE ONE AND THEN....

QUICK!! - CUDDLE HER BEFORE SHE'S GONE!!!

BAM, BAM, BANG!... BAM, BAM, BANG... BAM, BANGG!

YAWNNN SMAK SMAK

MHHHH

I FORGOT TO TELL YOU, HONEY... THEY'RE WORKING ON THE ROOF TODAY!

BAM, BANG, BANG BAM..... WHACKKKK!.....BANG, BANG, BANG!

OH, WOW! THEY'VE GOT THE ROOF UP ALREADY!

THIS IS GONNA BE MY PARENTS' NEW BEDROOM, DAWN—MY MOM HAS ALREADY CHANGED HER MIND 100 TIMES ABOUT THE BATHROOM!

FINALLY, YESTERDAY, SHE DECIDED TO HAVE THE TUB HERE, AND THE SINK AND TOILET OVER THERE.

WHY OVER THERE?

...'CAUSE THAT'S WHERE WE PUT THE *@*☆ PIPES!

EXCUSE ME... ARE THESE THE WALLS AROUND THE LINEN CLOSET?

OUI, MADAME.

OH,'CAUSE I WAS WONDERING IF WE COULD MAKE IT WIDER.—WE HAVE ALREADY THE DOORS...BUT, IF YOU WANT IT WIDER, OK!

I CHANGED THE VANITY TOP AND THE FIXTURES—AND WE ADDED A LIGHT IN THE SHOWER, LIKE YOU ASKED.

TSK—WHY DO THESE RENOVATIONS ALWAYS COST MORE THAN YOU EXPECT THEM TO?!!

$ $ $

BILL

THIS IS IT, JOHN—WE'VE MADE TWO VISITS TO THE DAY CARE CENTER, AND TODAY I'M LEAVING APRIL ON HER OWN.

HEALTH

DOES SHE KNOW?

NOT YET... I THOUGHT WE'D JUST GO AND I'D QUIETLY LEAVE WHEN SHE'S NOT LOOKING.

APRIL? HONEY? LET'S GO!.....WHERE'S APRIL, LIZ?

SHE QUIETLY LEFT WHEN YOU WEREN'T LOOKING.

NO! STAY WIF ME!

JUST LEAVE HER. SHE'LL BE FINE.

HOWLLLL MAMAAAA!

MAMA'S GONE, HONEY BUT SHE'LL BE BACK SOON.

MAMA... GONE?

UH HUH!

OH.

THINGS ARE CHANGING AROUND US SO FAST, EL. MIKE'S 17, LIZ IS IN JUNIOR HIGH—AND NOW APRIL'S IN DAY CARE!

EVEN OUR HOUSE IS CHANGING!

DOESN'T IT SEEM TO YOU THAT WE'RE IN A SORT OF TIME WARP—WHERE EVERYTHING IS CHANGING BUT US?

WHAT?

.....NEVER MIND.